Home and Away

Home and Away

Poems by

Jean L. Kreiling

© 2025 Jean L. Kreiling. All rights reserved.
This material may not be reproduced in any form, published,
reprinted, recorded, performed, broadcast,
rewritten, or redistributed without
the explicit permission of Jean L. Kreiling.
All such actions are strictly prohibited by law.

Cover design by Shay Culligan
Cover photo by Jean L. Kreiling

ISBN: 978-1-63980-760-4
Library of Congress Control Number: 2025938188

Kelsay Books
502 South 1040 East, A-119
American Fork, Utah 84003
Kelsaybooks.com

To my wise and witty brother,
William R. Kreiling (1960–2023),
with whom I always felt at home
and who was taken away too soon.

Acknowledgments

I am grateful to the editors of the following publications, in which many of the poems in this book first appeared, some under different titles or in slightly different versions.

Anacapa Review: "Home and Away," "Thirst at Three p.m."
Antiphon: "The Need for Clouds"
Autumn Sky Poetry: "Beach Walk with Friend and Stones," "The Glassmakers"
Better than Starbucks: "The Job at the Diner"
Birchsong: Poetry Centered in Vermont: "Wishing for Snow"
Crab Orchard Review: "At the Cliffs of Moher," "At the Realtor's Office," "Kitchen Cabinet Game"
The Edge City Review: "The Landowner at Middle Age"
Ekphrastic Review: "Cyclist and Crow," "Summer Porch," "Woman Carrying Canoe"
Light: "Dishwasher"
Lighten Up Online: "Ovillejo of the Short-Order Cook"
Literary Nest: "After Reading Hemingway Late at Night"
Mezzo Cammin: "The Old Stone Church," "Treasures," "Winter Greetings on the Walking Trail"
New England Poetry Club: "Home"
New Verse News: "The Flag Outside a Neighbor's Door"
Plough: "After Helping My Father Rake the Leaves"
Poetry by the Sea: "Calling Hours at the Funeral Home"
Pulsebeat Poetry Journal: "Triptych on Time in Northern Arizona," "Unreliable Witness"
Snakeskin: "Bajan Lust," "Her Coat Closet Inventory"
'Tis the Season: An Anthology of Christmas Poems: "Deck the Halls"

Several of the poems in this collection were honored in competitions:

"After Helping My Father Rake the Leaves" was short-listed for the Rhina Espaillat Poetry Award.
"After Reading Hemingway Late at Night" won Honorable Mention in the Kim Bridgford Memorial Sonnet Crown Contest.
"Calling Hours at the Funeral Home" won the Kim Bridgford Memorial Sonnet Contest.
"Home" won the New England Poetry Club's Samuel Washington Allen Prize.
"The Need for Clouds" was a finalist for the Frost Farm Prize.

Contents

I. At Home

The Landowner at Middle Age	17
Her Coat Closet Inventory	18
Kitchen Sonnets	19
On the Sofa	23
Treasures	24
La Talaverita, Sunday Morning NY Times	26
Summer Porch	27
Staircase Advice	28
Deck the Halls	29
After Reading Hemingway Late at Night	30

II. At Home Outdoors

Beside the Mud Puddle	37
Caterpillar	38
Beach Walk with Friend and Stones	39
To the Bird with the Gimlet Eye	41
Cyclist and Crow	42
Woman Carrying Canoe	43
The Contest	44
The Need for Clouds	45
Raindrop	46
Sun	47
After Helping My Father Rake the Leaves	48
Wishing for Snow	49
Winter Greetings on the Walking Trail	50

III. Around Town

Contemplating Time at the Corner Market   53
The Job at the Diner   55
Ovillejo of the Short-Order Cook   56
At the Realtor's Office   57
Thirst at Three p.m.   58
The Flag Outside a Neighbor's Door   59
Look Don't Look   60
Calling Hours at the Funeral Home   61
The Old Stone Church   62
Home and Away   63
Unreliable Witness   64

IV. Away

Snapshots of the Shining Sea Bikeway   69
At the Fisherman's Memorial   70
The Glassmakers   71
A Walk in Chicago   72
Hang Gliding at Jockey's Ridge   73
Triptych on Time in Northern Arizona   74
Bajan Lust   77
At St. Martin-in-the-Fields   79
At the Cliffs of Moher   80
The Thinkers   81
Two Birds Flying Beside a Cruise Ship   82
The Great Wave off Kanagawa   83

V. Home

Home   87

I
At Home

The Landowner at Middle Age

Just half an acre—maybe less—is all
that he can claim to own, but he surveys
his grass and trees, and hardly can recall
the grand imaginings of younger days,
when half would never do. His wants were vast:
the biggest house, the fastest car, the most
extreme adventures, taking him well past
the breakers and the tree lines; he would boast
of living on the edge, without a net.
But now he contemplates his home and yard,
maintained and paid for with decades of sweat,
and finds the old dreams easy to discard.
He'd never have imagined it at twenty,
but half an acre—maybe less—is plenty.

Her Coat Closet Inventory

puffy black parka
bulky as winter is long
slick as a cold heart

Henry's hiking boots
nudging her much smaller ones
he's not coming back

cap knitted by Gram
seed-stitched teal stripe on navy
warm as memory

thin dollar-store gloves
fraying at the fingertips
penny-wise mistakes

NPR tote bag
ready to bear books, bread, phone,
her share of bad news

Kitchen Sonnets

1. Young Pancake Chef

   for Tommy

He patiently observes, atop his stool,
as I spoon out the first pancake-to-be.
It's his turn next, and he observes the rule—
don't touch the griddle!—as he eagerly
takes up the ladle, lets the batter drip
and form a circle, hears a little hiss,
observes the bubbles. Then it's time to flip
the almost-pancake, and it's really this
that's magic: though it's not quite syrup-ready,
it's morphing from wet batter into food.
He makes some more, his technique sure, hand steady.
His grin suggests an artist's attitude;
the pleasure that the pancakes' taste gives later
can't beat the beaming pride of a creator.

2. Dishwasher

O merciful magician, who erases
the evidence of all my gluttony!
You drown the cookie crumbs, swallow the traces
of Chardonnay, inhale the bits of brie.
I hear your swishing, splashing incantation,
the holy water swirling through the crud—
but I can leave the room: no supplication
or kneeling is required, no sweat, no blood.
At cycle's end, a look inside reveals
that if I'm not quite cleansed of sin, at least
my dishes are. From my unbalanced meals,
I'm as good as absolved, and with no priest.
I've managed to gain spotless grace and hope
by tithing just a little pod of soap.

3. Kitchen Cabinet Game

It matters to me, much more than it should,
that drinking glasses stand sorted by size,
that bowls are neatly nested, that my good
dessert plates sparkle in their stack. The prize
that perfect order grants is hard to name.
It isn't peace, exactly, but a sort
of temporary triumph in a game
that never ends, played not on field or court
but on these shelves, a three-dimensional
ungridded Scrabble board where dishes make
the words, unspellable but meaningful;
a plate misplaced means an unsettling break
in symmetry and sense. Neatness may not
win much, but there are times it's all I've got.

4. Things My Mother Taught Me

She never taught me how to fry an egg,
the best way to cook yellow squash or peas,
what makes a crisp but tender chicken leg,
a recipe for creamy mac and cheese.
She didn't want us underfoot; she needed
to be efficient. She taught school, took classes,
took care of all of us—and she succeeded
at everything, including her molasses
cookies, which she did teach me to bake.
I watched her work hard and look out for those
she loved; I learned from her a way to make
a life, if not lasagna—and she chose
to teach me that to make a life complete,
sometimes you have to cook up something sweet.

On the Sofa

We were sitting here on the sofa—
I had just asked you *Want a beer?*—
when you said *Damn,* not to me
but to your buzzing phone,
then swiped its dark face,
said *Hi;* I heard
your mom say
*Your dad
died,*
and you
turned so pale
that it seemed death
had sat down with us,
claiming way too much space,
and might ask for its own beer.
That was months ago. You still weep,
and we both still hate this damned sofa.

Treasures

He'd never understood it—why these bits
of colored glass aroused in her such fits
of longing, followed by the acquisition
of pretty breakables. Her disposition,
not always sunny, brightened when she made
a sparkling work of art her own; he'd trade
an arm to see that smile. He'd watched her buy
a small red pitcher and a slender sky-
blue bud vase and a paperweight with pink
and yellow swirls and cups you couldn't drink
from (striped and speckled, frilled and fat and fluted)
and antique bottles, their shades mostly muted
(rose, lilac, and pale yellow like her hair),
and little bowls that held nothing but air.
He wondered why she loved these delicate
and useless things. Did these inanimate,
well-crafted, shiny objects make her feel
as if she shared their glow? In their ideal
designs did they remind her to be glad
for every pleasure, every gift she had?
Perhaps. He worried, though: it all could shatter,
and rainbows of detritus quickly scatter,
so easily. And then might her distress
cause something else to fracture? He'd confess
he didn't want to know; he would protect
whatever she deemed worthy to collect.
And so he built for her a sturdy case
designed to hold and show off every vase,
bowl, pitcher, paperweight, and cup. He knew
that her joy was his own, and he would do
his best to safeguard every frangible,
beloved, lovely thing—the tangible

bright baubles, her intangible delight,
and all the colors of each day and night
they shared. The case itself was mostly glass,
through which the always-shifting light could pass,
igniting every hue. The irony
did not escape him: these glass shelves could be
smashed, too. But so, he guessed, could everything;
you still love what or whom you love, you cling
to all that shines for you. And she was thrilled
with what he'd done; she kissed him and then filled
the case with treasures. It was no surprise
when he saw his own treasure in her eyes.

La Talaverita, Sunday Morning NY Times

after the painting by Aliza Nisenbaum (2016)

"La Talaverita" refers to Talavera ceramics, which feature intricate patterns and bright colors like those in the painting's background.

This blue room calms us as we sprawl and read
the *Times* together: we can face our fear
of bad news side by side. Though wars proceed,
this blue room calms us as we sprawl and read—
my hair loose, his hand on my leg. We need
each other to feel safe, as we do here;
this blue room calms us. As we sprawl and read
the *Times* together, we can face our fear.

Summer Porch

after the painting by Sally Storch (2012)

It looks so perfect, doesn't it?
My house, my porch, my chair, my book,
my dress—but take a closer look.
Both house and body have been knit
too tightly. In the symmetry
of arm and architecture, hard-
won compromises strain to guard
against collapse. Stability
became my prize when I could win
no other—faithful husband, child
to love—and so I'm reconciled
to night air on my desperate skin,
to peace like glass. From where I sit,
perfection's mostly counterfeit.

Staircase Advice

Take your time ascending this creaky staircase:
any step could grab at a toe and trip you,
bruise or break a tibia. Flesh is wobbly,
       spirit is willing.

Slowly rise, and sink into reminiscence
(hung beside you, photographs fracture rules of
time, the children home again); still, maintain your
       grip on the railing.

Fine things snap so easily, time degrading
things that ought to carry you—vows and plans and
bones—it's not so easy to keep on climbing
       rather than falling.

Deck the Halls

We dress the house in shiny clothes that spent
eleven months confined to cardboard cells
in attic jails. Parole for lights and bells
and plastic holly—like the mercy sent
to mortals when an infant slept in hay—
makes tangible our own inchoate hope:
we stretch to hang the garlands, and we grope
for virtues out of reach just yesterday.
The child became a man, did what he could,
and then died young—but gave a needy world
salvation. So each Christmas we've unfurled
these garments, draped them over glass and wood,
then packed them up, their clemency revoked,
our houses and refurbished souls uncloaked.

After Reading Hemingway Late at Night

My clean, well-lighted room was light too late,
the pages of my book far more appealing
than darkness and surrender to a state
of unengaged oblivion. But stealing
another hour for Hemingway may not
have been a wise choice. Though at last I've let
him go, he holds on: characters and plot
fill pages of my brain, his alphabet
too well-arranged to spell the spell of sleep.
And since I've missed the hour when eyes could close
and stay closed with the counting of some sheep—
their fleece can't muffle echoes of his prose—
I'm counting wives of Hemingway instead,
and wondering about the lives they led.

Four women married him. The lives they led—
the roles they played as Mrs. Hemingway—
must have been challenging. Had they misread
the man who'd leave them all? Each woman may
have thought that she had wed a different man,
since recent chapters in a life revise
what years have written. Each marriage began,
I'm sure, with hopes that it would not reprise
the previous debacle. But not one
would last more than a decade and a half,
each tale familiar: vows made and undone,
love doomed from the initial paragraph.
Write one true sentence was his famous creed;
truth written by the heart is hard to read.

The truth of one man's heart is hard to read,
but Hadley and young Ernest started out
(as lovers do) as if all they would need
was passion. I recall a time when doubt
or wariness could not corrupt my heart,
when my own Ernest—though his name was Jack—
slept here beside me. What broke us apart
is hardly worth recounting, but a lack
of passion wasn't it. We had our own
pale version of their Paris (the café
downtown); we too drank freely. If I'd known
how it would end—that Jack would soon betray
our bliss—I probably would still have lain
beside him, Hadley-like, bracing for pain.

Beside her husband, Hadley braced for pain,
and in time, his deceptions broke their bond.
How long can love and tolerance remain
when trust disintegrates, when you've been conned?
He left her for Pauline—well-educated,
a journalist. I can relate to her:
although I may be less sophisticated,
I too earned a degree; I too prefer
to write instead of watching someone write.
I wonder if I too would have felt free
to bed the married Hemingway. Tonight
I would have liked some manly company,
but as Pauline would learn, a man can make
a mess of things, make love seem a mistake.

Though Ernest left her, is it a mistake
to think him merely faithless? Macho code
or not, the men he wrote have hearts that break,
and so did he. Another episode
of short-lived marriage started in Key West,
where he met Martha. I wish I were there;
a warm salt breeze would surely help me rest,
and in the morning I might even dare
to drink a Bloody Mary with a stranger.
But Martha dared far more, and zealously:
courageous war reporter, she faced danger
repeatedly. She went to Normandy
on D-Day; she grew famous, well-respected—
and so, it seems, her husband felt neglected.

Maybe most wives and husbands feel neglected
at some point in their marriages; some days,
or years, leave spouses feeling disconnected
or undervalued. More than mere malaise,
it feels like the beginning of the end,
and sometimes it's exactly that, I've learned.
For Ernest, endings had become a trend—
beginnings, too, I guess, for he soon turned
to Mary, his fourth wife. Another writer,
twice wed herself, she must have understood
that he would not be easy: lover, fighter,
serial husband. But this marriage would
endure until the day Ernest could not—
until the moment Mary heard the shot.

The moment Mary heard the fatal shot
is one I can't imagine. I've known loss,
but not that fathomless abyss—the spot
a bullet finds—where grief and horror cross.
And though each new grief leaves a heart in pieces,
mine beats with a desire to keep on beating.
Until the chapter when my breathing ceases,
I'll keep the light on and I'll keep on reading—
and maybe counting: famous wives, the men
I've loved, true sentences, false vows. Hindsight
may favor caution, but the heart and pen
keep writing. And though I can't sleep tonight,
there's no one but myself to implicate:
my clean, well-lighted room was light too late.

II
At Home Outdoors

Beside the Mud Puddle

A small boy squats and wields a stick
to deftly probe the murk.
His mother captures, with a click,
a scientist at work.

The photo will immortalize
sharp knees, straw-colored hair,
and nut-brown puddle-focused eyes—
but not what they saw there

or how abruptly he dismissed
his task. She would deduce
that her mud-spattered scientist
was tired and wanted juice.

Caterpillar

two inches of fuzz
ooze down a five-year-old's arm:
the slither of spring

Beach Walk with Friend and Stones

for Barb, with thanks

I look for pretty shells—sun-paled and brittle,
the former homes of clams and scallops—bending
to claim them, as I did when I was little,
as if by grasping them, I'd be extending

my childhood by the sea. But here, the tides
deliver mostly stones—misshapen, gray—
and I dismiss them, though my friend decides
they're worth a look. She stops along our way

to pick up pebbles, and shows me a few.
They're oval, sharp-edged, red- or purple-flecked,
as pale as bones or water-marked with blue,
some flat enough to skip. Though I'd reject

them all, I nod and smile as she assesses
unlikely treasures. One, she notes, is pitted
with pinkish dents, one's heart-shaped, one she guesses
must come from Africa. She seems committed

to seeing more than gray, to celebrating
each small discovery. She pockets six
or seven, but her eye's discriminating;
she tosses most, and keeps a motley mix

of specimens, exhibiting each find
to me first on her palm. She discards one
whose gray is smudged with yellow—cloud combined
with just a bit of faded, unsure sun—

then waits as I walk back to rescue it.
I put it in my pocket: just a stone,
but salt-smoothed, depth-dimmed and yet subtly lit,
not by nostalgia but by grace unknown,

by time and tides that brought it to this shore.
My friend grins. Though our tastes don't quite align,
she knows that now I'll look a little more;
we both know that her vision has honed mine.

To the Bird with the Gimlet Eye

Plumage unremarkably gray and mottled,
tiny talons gripping a leafless tree limb,
songless, you were dull as a stone and staring.
    What were you thinking?

Gimlet eye occurred to me as I watched your
shiny black one challenging me to stare right
back, as still and patient and mute as you were,
    just as unblinking.

Why, I wondered, *gimlet?*—that's lime and vodka.
Now I've learned it's also a tool that pierces,
like that eye accusing me. Did you think I'd
    rather be drinking?

Cyclist and Crow

after the painting by Alex Colville (1981)

She seems relaxed. She pedals her Peugeot
with sneakered ease, but stares across the field
to watch the bird outpacing her. Although
she seems relaxed, she pedals her Peugeot
not quite as effortlessly as the crow
appears to glide; she's earthbound, though two-wheeled.
She seems relaxed—she pedals her Peugeot
with sneakered ease—but stares across the field.

Woman Carrying Canoe

after the painting by Alex Colville (1972)

The image isn't lewd; it doesn't bare
her breasts or bottom. But it bothers me
that we don't see her head—eyes, mouth, and hair.
The image isn't lewd—it doesn't bare
what should be private—but we don't see where
her thoughts unfold, just limbs flexed forcefully.
The image isn't lewd—it doesn't bare
her breasts or bottom—but it bothers me.

The Contest

He stood all morning on the pier
in stingy sun, clouds hovering;
his patience knew no limits here
beside the bay.

His focus never wavering,
he gripped the bamboo pole and stared,
his blue-gray eyes examining
the blue-gray bay.

The bamboo arched, the water stirred,
his unseen prey tightened the line,
and soon he pulled what he had lured
out of the bay.

And then he knelt to redefine
the win: unhooked his slimy prize—
its rippled scales and blue-gray shine
matching the bay—

and tossed it back in. As his eyes
grew brighter—now more blue than gray—
he saw nothing that he'd revise
beside the bay.

The Need for Clouds

The best fair skies are smudged with clouds, the kind
whose pure white amplifies and flatters blue,
the composition expertly designed
by airy impulse or a godly cue.
We need those puffy shapes, their boundaries
defining otherwise unsculpted space,
imposing onto its enormities
some finite contours that the eye can trace.
A hard blue bowl of sky boasts endlessness
too boldly, but grows soft and affable
when graced with scoops of sugary confection
that satisfy our lowborn faithlessness:
the smudges make skies comprehensible
to grounded mortals who mistrust perfection.

Raindrop

A
tiny
life,
a fast
fall. Un-
salted twin
of a tear. One
degree away from
a snowflake. One drip
in a window's translucent
Jackson Pollock. Catch it on
the tongue, catch it in a pot of
geraniums, catch it in a drainage
ditch. Sing it on a plain in Spain, on
a night in Georgia, with a lamppost.
Deflected by umbrellas, smeared by
windshield wipers, swallowed by
thirsty soil. Cursed, celebrated.
A bit more than a bit
of drizzle.

Sun

As soothing as a
pair of fleshy, well-loved arms
embracing a doubt-chilled soul at last,
or a swallow of chamomile tea seeping through
veins too long suffused with bitterness or February,
or the helpless laughter of a toddler surprised by the sea
lapping at feet over which his command is still tentative,
the sun executes its annual reclamation of power and renews
its dedication to heating as well as lighting the world beneath it,
resuming its command in an unelected and unchallenged position,
doing so with a grandmotherly grace, an old friend's confidence—
clearly a benevolent despot—until, blazing with a gassy smugness,
it crosses a line (frequently this happens around the Fourth of July,
but sometimes weeks earlier or later, its ruthlessness intensified by
its unpredictability), now not only insisting on its sovereignty but
also demonstrating sadistic tendencies, escalating from shining
to glaring, from soothing to baking to searing, then burning
with a passion more closely aligned with violence than
with affection, and though this despot faces a term
limit, that hardly matters when the soul groans,
the veins boil, the toddler sweats and
wails and will not nap, because
it's too damned hot.

After Helping My Father Rake the Leaves

First, I took a running leap,
and then, half buried in the heap
that we'd raked up, I lingered, caught
in a cocoon of leaves and thought.
I still remember how they smelled,
those castoffs autumn winds had felled—
both old and fresh, both wild and clean,
the sweet decay of summer's green;
and how they looked—small flags half-furled,
hot colors from a chilling world.
I breathed more deeply for a few
enchanted seconds. More leaves flew
as Dad watched, leaning on his rake.
He must have known what seasons take.
Leaves bright as fire broadcast their dark
reminder: beauty was a spark
that couldn't last, the freshened breath
of autumn air foreshadowed death.
But even so, my father grinned
and turned his face into the wind.
Years later, I'd learn just how brave
my father was, and how a wave
of chill or doubt could leave him caught
in his own grim cocoon of thought.
A darkness stalked him, but he lit
bright fires of love and work and wit,
and faced the wind, and found his way
for decades past that autumn day.
And now I kindle every flash
of memory that warms the ash
of loss. I see his profile still,
and face my autumns with his will.

Wishing for Snow

If only winter's knife-edged cold would bend
and break and finally disintegrate
in tiny crystal fragments, we'd defend
our driveways and our walks, and celebrate
our strength. If only this unyielding sky
would soften and dissolve into a mist
of icy flakes, we'd raise an awestruck eye
to watch their fall. But winter likes to twist
the knife, to maximize its penetration
and coolly signal its supremacy,
withholding postcard-pretty compensation
for its cold shoulder—broad but bitterly
unbending. Empty, numbing air says *no:*
no winter wonderland this time. No snow.

Winter Greetings on the Walking Trail

Plymouth, Massachusetts

We seldom say more than a word or two,
but seasons color our brief courtesy:
our winter words are meaningful, though few.

Cold-weather greetings often hint at who
and where we are: pride and tenacity
emerge from no more than a word or two.

Someone says *Brisk!* or *Crisp!*—a terse review,
not a complaint, and called out cheerfully—
a boast about our sturdiness. A few

will mutter *Stay warm!* in a pithy clue
to our New England solidarity:
we care, if brusquely. In a word or two,

we might affirm that fashion and hairdo
mean little: *Nice hat!* (In reality,
the earflaps look absurd.) I've heard a few

laments—once *Hurry, spring!*—and yes, it's true
that sometimes we just nod, so cold that we
can't sacrifice an extra breath or two.
Our winter words are meaningful, but few.

III
Around Town

Contemplating Time at the Corner Market

At ten a.m., few patrons walk these aisles;
slow footsteps on the cracked but well-swept tiles
announce my regulars. No one will buy
a lot at this hour, and I always sigh
to see these older customers. They're all
a little wobbly, and I fear they'll fall.
From my cashier's post, I watch them arrive—
each one on foot, none deft enough to drive:
the wrinkled lady who needs jam and tea,
the man whose dog looks better fed than he,
two well-coiffed matrons studying the greens.
A young man runs in, wearing tee-shirt, jeans,
and Red Sox cap, and grabs a Gatorade;
the air itself relaxes once he's paid
and left. It isn't that he posed a threat;
it's only that his tattooed arms upset
the morning's tone of sensible reserve,
his rushing feet seemed likely to unnerve
the old man's dog, and, well, the young man's speed
was futile. He, too, will one day concede
to time. The wrinkled lady scours her purse
for change; it seems to me her limp is worse.
And soon the man who's too thin for his clothes
will say again that Stop & Shop should close
its doors to rude folks, not good dogs; he'll frown
as he pays for his canned beef stew. *This town
ain't what it used to be,* he'll grumble. Then
the matrons will approach to ask me when
the produce was delivered; they'll debate
its freshness and its price, and calculate
how much they need—these two all business,
but they greet me by name: it's not *Oh, Miss!*

but *Good day, Jane!* The morning clientele
needs time to shop, and manages time well:
they take care with their choices and their canes,
consult coupons in resolute campaigns
to save, and squint to read lists that display
their spidery cursive. Later today,
pre-dinner customers will crowd this place,
buy bread and oat milk at a frantic pace
because they've run out—didn't plan ahead—
almost too busy to keep families fed.
Of course, I'm glad to see them. They will fill
the sometimes frighteningly empty till,
keep me employed—but when I say *hello,*
they barely nod; they swipe their cards and go.
Still, I don't judge them—and the time will fly
as they dash in and out and multiply
the market's income. But I do prefer
the ten a.m. scene: not much will occur,
but every moment counts. It's when this store
can fill an old man's needs with Dinty Moore,
a lady's with Red Rose; when small chores done
ensure that someone's day is well-begun;
when sun streams through plate glass, illuminating
cracked tiles, white hair, and well-stocked shelves awaiting
a shopper's scrutiny; when fresh romaine
means two stern matrons will chirp, *Good day, Jane!*

The Job at the Diner

He pulls the plastic lever on the urn
he cleaned an hour before, and holds a mug
to catch the dark brown liquid; he'll return
to this chore many times. He'll also lug
gray bins of dirty dishes to the back,
and wipe up spills of cereal and juice
and worse, and fetch more syrup for a stack
of pancakes drowned in it, and take abuse
from Old Man Atkins—and throughout, he'll smile.
No, this is not his dream job, and he yearns
for better, but why not do it with style?
He knows that he's much more than what he earns.
Sometimes what keeps your day from being hell
is doing what you do extremely well.

Ovillejo of the Short-Order Cook

Eggs, waffles, pancakes, eggs again—
by ten,
I've come to hate the waiter's call.
I'm all
worn out, I'm bored; I'd like to hide,
but fried
potatoes, ham, grits on the side—
they're duties that I cannot shirk.
Though grateful to have steady work,
by ten, I'm all but fried.

At the Realtor's Office

They're selling dreams, they like to say;
their storefront photographs display
the pricey, well-staged fantasies
they call *rare opportunities*
and *gems*. They hope you'll overpay

for your townhouse, ranch, or chalet,
your *great investment,* your doorway
to debt. You're lured in by degrees:
they're selling dreams

of closet space, kitchens *(gourmet!),*
and pride. Why shouldn't wants outweigh
misgivings and realities?
The realtors ply their expertise,
and you're an easy mark to sway—
they're selling dreams.

Thirst at Three p.m.

There are so many bars in this town—
one known for wine, one for danger,
three within walking distance.
She pushes the stroller
past Hometown Tavern,
then Paddy's Pub,
and she's so
thirsty,
but
the kid
is whining,
warming up for
a tantrum, no doubt;
he won't nap anymore,
isn't lulled by squeaky wheels,
might make a spectacular scene
that would slake some tipsy gossip's thirst.

The Flag Outside a Neighbor's Door

As they pulled the officer down the stairs, face down, another rioter beat him with an American flag as the mob chanted "USA! USA! USA!"
—The New York Times, *January 11, 2021*

Just down the street, outside a neighbor's door,
it reaches up and out, as if for hope
or heaven, in an effort to restore
its honor and resist the downward slope
traversed by those who lied, who followed liars,
who beat a man with those same stripes and stars,
who lit and fanned and spread murderous fires
that left some dead, the rest of us with scars.
I see Old Glory fluttering in the breeze—
but elsewhere, desecrated by a gang
of thugs, it symbolized not liberties
and laws, but rage, and justice by flash-bang.
I miss the days when I was confident
about what flags by neighbors' front doors meant.

Look Don't Look

a granite-faced cop
a silent red ambulance
no one's hurrying

a uniformed arm
waves my SUV along
nothing to see here

single red sneaker,
contorted bike, dented truck
plot details askew

my eyes straight ahead
my eyes drifting to the wreck
too much to see here

Calling Hours at the Funeral Home

He wants to be here—it's for his Aunt Lou,
who baked him cookies, sent him cards and money,
applauded his good news from first grade through
the senior partnership, and called him *honey*
to her last day. But this grim atmosphere
could not be further from Aunt Lou: his nose
detects old carpet, men's cologne, and fear,
instead of nutmeg, lavender, and rose.
He stays a while—shakes hands and murmurs, tries
not to inhale too much—until he thinks
Aunt Lou would probably have rolled her eyes
and told him *Go!* He pulls his coat on, winks
at Aunt Lou's portrait, leaves. Outside, it's cold;
he sucks in all the air his lungs will hold.

The Old Stone Church

The stone it's made of testifies
to something close to permanence;
façades, however, can be lies.

It houses faith and eloquence,
the prayers and homilies devout
despite the meager evidence.

True faith demands we trust without
a shred of proof, and may achieve
great miracles, though there's some doubt.

Stone shelters those who hope and grieve
and celebrate what never dies.
Some say the faithful are naïve,
and some, the lucky ones, believe.

Home and Away

for Bill

My ears ring with the treble roar of eight-
year-olds; one hits the ball, I watch it fly,
a kid runs with my brother's hungry gait—
but no one's on this field as I walk by.

I'm three blocks from my house, but also three
states distant, five decades ago. A map
or calendar disproves this, but I see
my brother's curls escaping from his cap.

Unreliable Witness

Yes, I walk by here every evening, right
around this time. I'm no voyeur, but yes,
their picture window draws my eye—a bright,
broad frame for family portraits. I confess
that I've looked forward to that moment when
I turn the corner onto Pinewood Court
and see the intimate tableau again:
mom, dad, a son, a daughter—just the sort
of neighbors you would want—a scene of cozy
companionship as they relaxed together,
watched TV, or played board games. I'm not nosy
enough to stare—I couldn't tell you whether
they played Yahtzee or Trivial Pursuit—
I just kept walking my accustomed route.

Some summer evenings brought them all outside,
the grownups watching as the children ran
and laughed. The parents seemed to take great pride
and pleasure in their happy little clan.
And when I walked this way in autumn's chill,
I gazed at that big window jealously,
just wishing that their warmth and cheer could spill
out here along with lamplight. I could see
them sitting side by side to read or chat;
once I heard music, and I saw them dance;
they never even seemed to have a spat.
A troubled home, you ask? Oh, not a chance.
I saw no trace of tension or distress;
no tragedy could lurk at this address.

But last night as I walked along this street,
the picture window framed only the dad,
the tableau noticeably incomplete.
How did he look? Well, fine . . . I think he had
a drink in one hand. Yes, I wondered where
the others were. I wasn't worried, though—
I'd never seen a hint of danger there.
I didn't stop; I had two miles to go.
And then tonight, I walk into this scene:
the dad handcuffed, lights flashing red and blue,
an ambulance—not rushing—does that mean
the worst? Officer, did I miss some clue?
Sometimes the children or their mother waved;
I didn't know they needed to be saved.

IV
Away

Snapshots of the Shining Sea Bikeway

North Falmouth to the Woods Hole ferry dock, Massachusetts

from sea to shining sea
　—*Katharine Lee Bates*

rusty bike pedals
air shiny with sun-crazed salt
the breeze sets your pulse

Vineyard Sound sapphire,
sand-spun gold, leaf-lively green
June's dream-brief palette

kids in pink helmets
pumping their sparkly sneakers
the season's experts

head-down spandex guy
counting miles and fat grams burned
barely sees the sea

you pause at the dock
floating hulks mosey away
you head back, buoyant

At the Fisherman's Memorial

Gloucester, Massachusetts

I barely swim; I lack the faintest notion
of how to helm a boat of any kind.
But sea salt in my veins has long aligned
my restless heartbeat with the wild commotion
of foaming breakers. Walking by the ocean,
I always breathe more deeply, and I find
much more than mere air. On this spot designed
to honor fishermen and their devotion
to labor in the roughest seas, I grieve
for those named here, who breathe no more, for whom
the sea meant danger, work, a battered keel.
My romance with the ocean seems naïve
before reminders of a salty tomb,
before this great bronze sailor at the wheel.

The Glassmakers

Simon Pearce Glass, Quechee, Vermont

for Jane, Kate, Maureen, and Sally

Five women watched as one man's breath inflated
the molten glass, one man spun it in flame,
one trimmed and shaped it. Expertly translated
by patient craftsmen, ash and sand became
a useful vessel and a work of art,
exhaled and fired and molded into being.
Each piece required each man to do his part,
a deft alliance nurturing and freeing
both elegance and strength. Each woman bought
a finished bowl that caught the autumn light
and scattered it—a slow-baked prize, well-wrought,
like their decades-long bond. With eyes as bright
as autumn sun and just as sure to fade,
they savored all that breath and warmth had made.

A Walk in Chicago

The wind had teeth; I felt its bite
draw tears. Beside the endless lake,
steel towers boasted sturdy height;
the city glittered at daybreak.

I cruised the river, shopped the Mile,
rode the L's roaring machine,
savored pizza Chicago-style,
admired great art, gawked at the Bean.

But my Chicago memories
are sharpest from those times I strolled
beside the lake. My eye still sees
that sparkle; I still feel the cold.

A broad right angle framed my view:
flat water, skyscrapers upright.
But wild air could nudge both, I knew;
the wind had teeth. I felt its bite.

Hang Gliding at Jockey's Ridge

Nags Head, North Carolina

The giant near-bird launches nimbly,
catches currents of sea-drunk air,
adroitly soars, dips, and glides—
but then lands with a thud
and a stumbling run,
sighs with relief,
and slips off
its bright
wings.

Triptych on Time in Northern Arizona

1. The Red Rocks of Sedona

They're red as rust, but not the rust
of swift disintegration—
not telegraphing *dust to dust*
or imminent expiration.

This is the red of iron fated
to outlast us all;
we're fascinated by translated
mud now standing tall.

Seas rose and fell, wind layered sand
in distant yesterdays.
These rocks might help us understand
that we are just a phase.

2. Grand Canyon Time

The face of earth shows here deep furrows cut
in inexplicable geometry
by water, wind, and time. Chasms abut
the mile-high mesas layered garishly
in signs of age; each hour of light repaints
the rocky canvas. Humbled mortals, small
and short-lived as we are, trapped in constraints
not quite fathomed before, can't grasp it all;
despite our vaunted wisdom, we can't know
what sandstone knows. But if we're wise, we see
in human faces sculpted by time's flow
another grandeur: breath's own history.
Composed of rock or flesh, each face betrays
time's price, recouped in an admirer's gaze.

3. Route 66, Seligman

> *The beginning of the decline for US 66 came in 1956 with the signing of the Interstate Highway Act. . . . It was officially removed from the United States Highway System in 1985 after it was entirely replaced by segments of the Interstate Highway System.*
> —*"U.S. Route 66," Wikipedia*

> *Get your kicks on Route 66.*
> —*Bobby Troup*

To stop here is to turn the clock hands back
to Elvis mania and Chevy grilles.
This road was once the only beaten track;
this town saves what the interstate can't kill.

Sorry, we're OPEN! says a neon sign,
beside a notice that *You can have cheese
on your cheeseburger!* Lewder quips define
the decor of restroom facilities.

A menu offers malts and tacos—and
dead chicken—would you eat the other kind?
Used napkins are an option—but demand
new ones; these nice folks will oblige, you'll find.

It's part nostalgia and it's part bad jokes
that probably have never been in style.
Seligman holds its ground, and gamely cloaks
its downturn in bright turquoise and a smile.

Bajan Lust

Bajan (BĀ-juhn): of or relating to Barbados or its inhabitants

In swells of wet persuasion, sun-
drunk ocean licks the yielding sand,
recedes, returns again, affirms
the endless lust of sea for land.

The air is sultry here, the food
a spicy sharpness on the tongue,
the Bajan speech a rich dessert
of open vowels warmly sung.

Rum lubricates the island life,
and sugarcane grows tall and sweet,
but neither earns enough; they can't
shore up the Bajan balance sheet.

The streets are patchy, sidewalks crumble,
tiny wooden houses rot.
A guest leaves natives guilt-grand tips,
for guests are nearly all they've got.

The Spanish and the Portuguese
and then the English claimed this place;
now proudly free, the island knows
its glory lies in the embrace

of two great oceans, lovers both—
Atlantic and Caribbean—
one wilder, one more turquoise, but
each equally a guardian

and greedy swain. Each keeps its coast
astir, effulgent, satisfied—
an old romance in Bajan blues:
the constant ardor of the tide,

these swells of wet persuasion. Sun-
drunk ocean licks the yielding sand
again, again, and proves again
the endless lust of sea for land.

At St. Martin-in-the-Fields

church in London, England

Past Trafalgar's lions, past
Nelson perched on his
granite mast,

I found humbler space, and heard
at my pew no roar,
not a word

of martial triumph—instead,
heaven-hewn song that
could have led,

I was sure, to peace
for all beasts.

At the Cliffs of Moher

on Ireland's Atlantic coast

Ahead of me, three dozen tourists climbed
against a roaring wind that had defeated
two dozen more. I struggled, each step timed
to dodge a gust, as my resolve competed
with waves of air so stout and strong they made
my every halting stride a revelation
of my own smallness. But my eyes repaid
my legs and lungs—the cliffs an illustration
of time itself. Seas crashed against their faces,
gales howled as earth stood motionless and mute,
and at the peak I seemed to inhale traces
of something pure and ancient. From the brute
magnificence of earth and air and sea,
I drew old strength and new humility.

The Thinkers

*after a photo of a young boy and his father seated at the foot of
Rodin's* The Thinker *in the Rodin Sculpture Garden, Paris*

The thinkers—there are three of them—all sit
in Paris sun, engaged in contemplation
that might be genuine or counterfeit,
two of them clearly posed in imitation
of Rodin's massive man, but all the same
immortalized, like him, by camera clicks.
Each one of them deserves the sculpture's name,
although we can't know what ideas might fix
each thinker's posture: what the artist meant,
the boy imagines, or the grown man feels.
We do know that each head bowed, each back bent,
and each right hand just slightly clenched reveals
what thinking can produce: great art, good fun,
immortal moments in the Paris sun.

Two Birds Flying Beside a Cruise Ship

for Salil

Their course has not been charted by the man
who steers this vessel; their species has flown
this air for generations, their flight plan
arranged by instincts known to wings alone.
But it does look as if these two intend
to keep us company—speed calibrated
to match our own, a path that doesn't bend
from ours. Their constancy has captivated
the handful of us at the rail—despite
the likelihood that it's not loyalty,
but mostly habit (and perhaps the sight
of food scraps) that keeps them reliably
beside us—and with hearts afloat, we trace
imagined ties to their unswerving grace.

The Great Wave off Kanagawa

after the woodblock print by Katsushika Hokusai,
No. 1 from Thirty-Six Views of Mt. Fuji (1831)

The wave's enormity insists
its impact will be great;
this woodblocked moment, though, resists
its force. The eye will wait

in vain to see what's next; a master
made the breaker stall
precisely on its cusp. Disaster
may or may not fall.

Three boats will spend eternity
imperiled but not crushed
by wet kinetic energy.
The ocean's roar is hushed

as foam and salt stay where they are:
unchanging blue and white
in crests that dwarf Mt. Fuji, far
away in shadowed light.

Despite momentum's robust claim,
no future's ever known;
at most, the present, just one frame,
is all we ever own.

This water rose, began to curl,
then paused. No one can make
its perfect, potent arc unfurl
or know how it will break.

V
Home

Home

The tiny place could barely hold their wealth:
Salvation Army table, mismatched chairs,
curb-rescued sofa, happiness, good health,
and callow confidence that love like theirs
would never fail, and they would surely thrive
on romance; feeding on a gritty mix
of poverty and passion, they'd survive.
That confidence, of course, would never fix
the landlord's balky furnace. But they found
a bed they could afford, and heaven couldn't
have held more bliss. The loud, unlovely sound
of traffic out their rattling windows wouldn't
drown out the conversation they'd begun,
the words and silences that made them one.

The words and silences that made them one
gave voice to ordinary dreams: they'd find
a house to buy, one with a yard, and sun
would always shine on them. The day they signed
the papers, they were nervous, but enchanted
by their new place—a house with drafty rooms
(all needing paint), few closets, floors that slanted,
a lawn choked by dead dandelion blooms.
But this young couple knew what really mattered:
not sagging porch steps, but the heady scent
of lilacs shading them; not pipes that clattered,
but their own chatter during evenings spent
beside the soot-stained hearth; not slanting floors,
but all the joy that lived inside the doors.

But all the joy that lived inside the doors
did not prevent them from imagining
still more. Their newly finished corridors
soon hosted little feet, and everything
they did to renovate would never meet
the needs of four rambunctious kids. And so
the couple and their brood moved to a street
of spacious newer homes. The kids would grow
up quickly here, through noisy, busy years
of Scrabble in the paneled den, tense fights
around the kitchen table, bitter tears
at teenage tragedies, and anxious nights
for parents waiting up. And this was where
they'd learn a dreadful truth: life wasn't fair.

They learned the dreadful truth: life wasn't fair—
and life, in fact, could end without a warning.
They lost their oldest child—the one who'd share
her cookie with a friend, who'd knelt one morning
beside the shrubbery to cut a sprig
of heather for her teacher, and who'd led
her siblings in freeze tag. Her heart was big,
and then it stopped. And it took every shred
of will they had to keep inhaling, keep
pretending they were still alive. But walls
that held their endless grief and heard them weep
would also bear framed photos of new calls
for celebration: birthdays, contests won,
three kids still growing, more time in the sun.

Three kids grew up, and more time in the sun
was what their parents wanted. They retired
and moved to Florida, glad to be done
with winter's mess. Although they still required
a house that gave them room enough to host
the kids, and soon the grandkids, and some land
for gardening, this new home by the coast
was easier to manage. They would stand
on their lanai (they liked the local word)
and watch the water, happy to be warm.
Though it got awfully hot when no breeze stirred
their quarter-acre, though a deadly storm
was often forecast, they were lucky. Fate
brought them new pleasures to appreciate.

New pleasures led them to appreciate
each other more, as well. And soon they knew
that all they needed, as their hour grew late
and years grew short, was just a place for two.
They bought a condo, small but well designed:
one floor, one bedroom, one small balcony,
and several grab bars. And they didn't mind
that some smug younger folks had cleverly
declared this neighborhood "God's waiting room";
they'd seldom sat and waited, wouldn't sit
and wait for death. Though they did not assume
they had a lot of time left, none of it
was likely to be idly squandered. No,
their dance continued, though their steps were slow.

Their dance continued, though their steps were slow,
and in another decade, slowed still more.
They both felt that they still had miles to go,
but they admitted they were tired and sore.
She needed pills that she could barely count;
he could no longer help her clean and cook.
More difficulties than they could surmount
alone led to their last new home: they took
one large room in "assisted living." Here
they joined a book club, and they made new friends.
They liked the smaller space—liked being near
each other all the time. And though their ends
were now approaching with a kindly stealth,
the tiny place could barely hold their wealth.

About the Author

Jean L. Kreiling is the author of three previous collections of poetry from Kelsay Books: *Shared History* (2022), *Arts & Letters & Love* (2018), and *The Truth in Dissonance* (2014).

Her work has been awarded the Rhina Espaillat Poetry Prize, the Kim Bridgford Memorial Sonnet Prize, the Frost Farm Prize for Metrical Poetry, the Able Muse Write Prize, two Laureates' Prizes in the Maria W. Faust Sonnet Contest, and three New England Poetry Club prizes, among other honors.

Kreiling is Professor Emeritus of Music at Bridgewater State University, and she formerly taught English at Western Carolina University. Her articles on the intersections between music and literature have been published in several academic journals. An Associate Poetry Editor for *Able Muse: A Review of Poetry, Prose & Art,* she lives on the coast of Massachusetts.

www.ingramcontent.com/pod-product-compliance
Lightning Source LLC
Chambersburg PA
CBHW030909170426
43193CB00009BA/790